W9-AUU-164

NUCLEAR ENERGY

By Nigel Saunders

Consultant: Suzy Gazlay, M.A.,
science curriculum resource teacher

Gareth Stevens
Publishing

Please visit our web site at: www.garethstevens.com
For a free color catalog describing Gareth Stevens Publishing's
list of high-quality books, call 1-800-542-2595 (USA) or
1-800-387-3178 (Canada).

Library of Congress Cataloging-in-Publication Data

Saunders, Nigel.
  Nuclear energy / Nigel Saunders.
    p. cm. — (Energy for the future and global warming)
  Includes index.
  ISBN: 978-0-8368-8402-9 (lib. bdg.)
  ISBN: 978-0-8368-8411-1 (softcover)
  1. Nuclear energy—Juvenile literature. 2. Nuclear power plants. I. Title.
QC792.S65   2008
621.48'3—dc22   2007008752

This edition first published in 2008 by
Gareth Stevens Publishing
A Weekly Reader® Company
1 Reader's Digest Road
Pleasantville, NY 10570-7000 USA

Copyright © 2008 by Gareth Stevens, Inc.

Produced by Discovery Books
Editors: Geoff Barker and Sabrina Crewe
Designer: Keith Williams
Photo researcher: Rachel Tisdale
Illustrations: Stefan Chabluk and Keith Williams

Gareth Stevens editor: Carol Ryback
Gareth Stevens art direction and design: Tammy West
Gareth Stevens production: Jessica Yanke

Photo credits: Nuclear Energy Institute: cover, title page. NASA: 6; / JPL 24.
istockphoto.com: / Melody Kerchhoff 7. Library of Congress: 12. CORBIS: 17.
Greenpeace: / Sergei Spasokukotskiy 20.

Printed in the United States of America

1 2 3 4 5 6 7 8 9 11 10 09 08 07

CONTENTS

Cover photo: The cooling tower of the Callaway Nuclear Plant releases harmless steam. The domed containment building in the background houses the nuclear reactor itself. The power plant, in Callaway County, Missouri, opened in 1984.

Words in **boldface** appear in the glossary or in the "Key Words" boxes within the chapters.

CHAPTER ONE

ENERGY AND GLOBAL WARMING

Electricity powers our lives. It lights and heats our houses, allows us to watch TV, dry our clothes, and ride in an elevator. The many ways we use electricity grows every year. The world's population is also growing, and all those extra people will need electricity. How can we produce enough electricity for everyone?

Fossil fuels

We must use the energy from a fuel source to produce electricity. Coal, crude oil, and natural gas are three basic (or primary) sources of energy. Electricity itself is a secondary source of energy because it is made from a primary fuel source.

Coal, oil, and natural gas are all fossil fuels — fuels formed in the ground millions of years ago. About two-thirds of the world's electricity is produced from the burning of fossil fuels. Fossil fuels are not **renewable**, however. Once we use them up, they will be gone forever. This is one reason we need to find other fuels to use to produce electricity.

Pollution from fossil fuels

There are other reasons to cut back on our use of fossil fuels. Fossil fuels give off gases when they burn. The gases **pollute** (dirty) the air, water, and land. Polluted air harms people who breathe it. Polluted

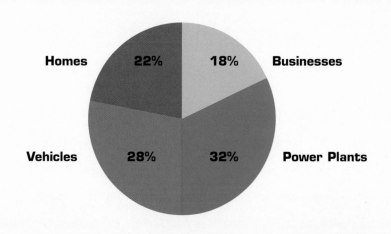

ENERGY USE IN THE UNITED STATES IN 2005

Homes 22%	18% Businesses
Vehicles 28%	32% Power Plants

This chart shows energy use in the United States. It shows how much energy was used by homes, businesses, **power plants**, and vehicles.

water evaporates into the air to form clouds and falls to Earth as acid rain, sleet, or snow. Acid rain, sleet, or snow can slowly kill plants and animals.

Blanket of air

Many gases form the atmosphere (the blanket of air around Earth). Some gases trap heat in the air. We call these **greenhouse gases**. They keep our planet warm enough for living things to exist. Water vapor, methane, and carbon dioxide are all greenhouse gases.

When we burn fossil fuels, we make extra greenhouse gases. When we burn fossil fuels, we add more greenhouse gases to the atmosphere. The amounts

Some spacecraft use nuclear energy to make electricity and keep their batteries warm at night. The Mars Exploration Rover Mission landed two vehicles on Mars in 2004.

"Of all our nation's energy sources, only nuclear power plants can generate massive amounts of electricity without emitting an ounce of air pollution or greenhouse gases. And thanks to the advances in science and technology, nuclear plants are far safer than ever before."

President George W. Bush, August 2005

of greenhouse gases in the air have increased in the last hundred years. Scientists believe this increase is causing Earth to get warmer. This changes the worldwide weather patterns, or climate. The effect of climate change is called **global warming**.

HEATING UP THE WORLD

Large areas of ice are melting at the North and South Poles. The extra water pouring into the oceans is causing worldwide rises in sea levels. In time, some cities and land along coasts may become flooded.

As the world warms up, rainfall patterns change. Forests and grasslands may become deserts. Food crops may fail. Plants and animals that cannot adapt to the changes may die out.

As a result of global warming, some places may receive less rain. Certain areas, like this watering hole in Africa, may shrink or dry up completely.

Other sources of energy

Each of us may be able to help slow global warming. We can burn fewer fossil fuels. We can find other sources of energy. Renewable energy is the best way to meet our increasing energy needs. Renewable sources, such as wind or solar power, never run out. Most renewable energy sources do not produce harmful gases. But we cannot make wind power on a calm day or use energy from the Sun when it is dark. How can we make plenty of electricity whenever it is needed? Nuclear energy might be one answer to our growing demand for electric power.

All about atoms

In order to understand how we make nuclear energy, we must learn a few things about **atoms**. We cannot even see the tiny atoms that make up everything around us. Atoms contain a huge amount of power. We know how to release that power and make electricity.

Nuclear energy has also been used to make bombs that killed many thousands of people. Because of that, many people are afraid of nuclear power. They worry that an accident at a nuclear power plant will give off harmful rays that can kill living things.

People also worry about global warming. They know scientists are trying to make the use of nuclear energy safer. People also know that our energy needs are growing. Nuclear power may be our energy for the future.

KEY WORDS

global warming: the gradual warming of Earth's climate
greenhouse gases: substances in the atmosphere that trap heat energy
pollute: to make land, air, or water dirty
renewable: having a new or reusable supply of material constantly available for use

CHAPTER TWO

POWER IN THE ATOM

Gasoline and other fuels produce heat energy when they burn. They release heat because of a chemical reaction. A chemical reaction causes a change, such as when two things mix.

Burning is a chemical reaction that combines a fuel with oxygen in the air.

Nuclear energy is different. It does not use chemical reactions. Instead, it uses **nuclear reactions**.

ENERGY IN A NUCLEAR REACTION

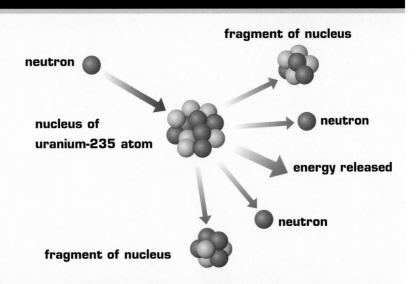

The diagram shows a nuclear reaction. A neutron is fired at an atom. The atom's **nucleus** splits and releases energy. It also releases more neutrons to hit other atoms. This releases extra amounts of energy.

SPLITTING THE ATOM

When a uranium atom splits, two or three neutrons break free of its nucleus. If one of these hits another uranium nucleus, that nucleus splits. This action releases more neutrons. These neutrons go on to split even more uranium nuclei. Countless uranium atoms quickly become part of the reaction. This process is called a **chain reaction**. The splitting of one atom does not release very much energy. A chain reaction, however, can release an enormous amount!

Inside the atom

Everything is made of atoms. Imagine atoms as tiny balls that are too small to see. It is hard to understand just how small they are. But if people were the same size as atoms, all the people in the world would fit in a box smaller than a pencil tip!

Inside an atom are even smaller parts. These particles are called protons, neutrons, and electrons.

The nucleus is made of protons and neutrons. The electrons circle around, or orbit, the nucleus. A nuclear reaction changes the makeup of the tiny nucleus at the center of the atom.

This type of reaction happens when the nucleus of an atom splits. It can also happen when the nuclei of atoms join together. Either of these reactions releases enormous amounts of energy.

Isotopes and radioisotopes

Some substances contain just one type of atom. These pure substances are known as **elements**.

Every atom of an element contains the same number of protons. Carbon atoms, for example, always contain six protons. Most carbon atoms have six neutrons, too. Some types of carbon are a little different, however. Their atoms may have a different number of neutrons. Carbon atoms can have between three and eleven neutrons. Atoms with varying numbers of neutrons are called **isotopes**.

The nuclei of some isotopes are unstable. This means that they can split apart easily. When a nucleus splits, it releases the nuclear energy stored inside the nucleus. Isotopes that produce nuclear energy are called **radioisotopes**.

NUCLEUS OF URANIUM-235 ATOM

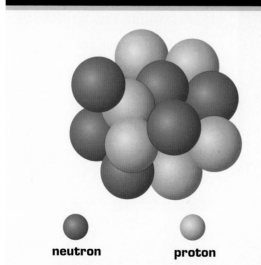

neutron   proton

This diagram shows a simplified version of an atom of uranium–235 (U–235), a very rare isotope. In reality, such an atom would have a total of 92 protons and 143 neutrons. Atoms of U–235 are extremely unstable. They split apart easily. Nuclear power plants use the U–325 isotope in their reactors to make electricity.

Radiation

So what is nuclear energy? It is energy released from a nucleus as heat, like heat from a fire. Heat is a kind of **radiation** — which means something that gives off energy in rays, or waves. Another name for heat is infrared radiation. It feels warm. Light is another form of radiation. It is made of rays and packets of energy called photons.

In 1896, French scientist Henri Becquerel discovered that uranium ore, called pitchblende, gave off radiation. Marie and Pierre Curie were scientists who worked with Becquerel in France. Marie Curie saw that radiation was not like a chemical reaction. She found that some elements naturally gave off radiation. She called these elements **radioactive**. The Curies studied

Marie Curie shared the 1903 Nobel Prize in Physics with Pierre Curie and Henri Becquerel for their work on radiation. Marie Curie was the first woman to win a Nobel Prize, and the first person to win two Nobel Prizes.

uranium for many years. They found two other radioactive metals. They named one polonium (after Poland, where Marie Curie was born). They named the other "radium" because it gives off lots of radiation.

Harmful radiation

Heat is not the only radiation that comes from nuclear energy. Other types of radiation are released during reactions, too. We cannot feel, see, smell, hear, or taste these kinds of nuclear radiation. But they are very dangerous. When people talk about radiation, they usually mean harmful radiation.

Radiation can damage or kill parts of our bodies. It can also make cancers

DANGEROUS RAYS

Alpha (α), beta (β), and gamma (γ) are the first three letters of the Greek alphabet. The letters are also the names of three dangerous forms of radiation. Each of these types of radiation has a different energy. Even though a sheet of paper can stop alpha rays, they are the most dangerous if they get inside our bodies. Beta radiation goes through paper, but can be stopped by aluminum foil. Gamma radiation travels right through paper and aluminum. It is only stopped by dense metals, such as lead, or thick concrete. All of these different forms of radiation can damage living organisms.

grow. High doses of radiation cause radiation poisoning. The poisoning causes people to get very sick. They often die.

The first scientists to study radioactive substances did not know that radiation was dangerous to their health. Marie Curie probably died from radiation. Today, people who work with radiation follow special safety rules.

Background radiation

Radiation is all around us. It is called background radiation and comes from different sources. Background radiation comes from space and from the ground. It is even in some foods and in drinking water. We cannot escape background radiation. Luckily, this natural radiation occurs in small amounts that do not cause health problems.

The amount of radiation produced by a nuclear chain reaction is much, much larger than background radiation. Radiation from an uncontrolled chain reaction can kill many people. Anyone who works with radioactive materials must be careful to use them safely.

KEY WORDS

isotope: an atom of an element that exists in varying forms, each with a different number of neutrons

nucleus: a cluster of neutrons and protons at the center of an atom. Two or more are called nuclei.

radiation: the energy given off as invisible waves and particles

radioisotopes: atoms that can produce radiation

CHAPTER THREE

ENERGY FROM A CHAIN REACTION

The Sun shines brightly in the sky because of nuclear reactions that take place within it. Deep inside Earth, much heat is also created by nuclear reactions. People have learned how to create controlled nuclear reactions to make energy that produces electricity.

Nuclear power plants

Scientists make nuclear energy in nuclear reactors. Nuclear reactors create, control, and contain nuclear reactions. The energy produced by the reactors makes electricity. Power plants using **nuclear reactors** make one-sixth of the world's electricity. Nuclear power plants make about one-fifth of all the electricity used in the United States.

In a **power plant**, fuel releases heat energy. Nuclear power plants create nuclear reactions that release heat energy. The heat boils water to make steam, just like a giant teakettle. The steam spins a turbine, an engine with blades. As the turbine's blades spin, they turn a shaft connected to a **generator**. It changes mechanical energy into electricity.

A chain reaction

A forest fire is another kind of a chain reaction. A small spark can start a few leaves on fire. The flames travel to the branches and then from tree to tree. More and more

NUCLEAR POWER

GOOD THINGS	PROBLEMS
No pollution or greenhouse gases created	Core produces radiation and radioactive wastes
Small amount of fuel needed	Natural U–235 very rare; must be made by people
Very efficient fuel source produces a lot of electricity relatively cheaply	Construction and safety costs for nuclear reactors very expensive; limited lifetime
Produces small amounts of waste	**Nuclear waste** remains dangerous for thousands of years; power plant life span limited

trees catch fire until everything in sight is burning. Some nuclear reactions are like a forest fire out of control. Once they get started, nothing can stop them.

An atomic bomb blast is an uncontrolled nuclear chain reaction. The bomb releases huge amounts of nuclear energy very quickly. A nuclear reactor controls the chain reaction. It runs at a steady pace all the time.

Inside the reactor

The nuclear reactor **core** is the heart of a nuclear power plant. It holds the nuclear fuel. An isotope of uranium, U–235, is most commonly used as the nuclear fuel in nuclear power plants.

The U–235 fuel is formed into small pellets. Each U–235 pellet is only about the size of your fingertip. But it produces about the same amount of energy as

The world's first atomic bomb was tested near Alamagordo, New Mexico, on July 16, 1945. To end World War II, the United States dropped two atomic bombs several weeks later on the Japanese cities of Hiroshima and Nagasaki. More than two hundred thousand people were killed. This huge, mushroom-shaped cloud is from the August 9 Nagasaki bombing.

LISE MEITNER (1878-1968)

Lise Meitner was born in Vienna, Austria, in 1878. In those days, it was rare for women to study science at college. Meitner studied physics at the University of Vienna. In 1907, she went to work at a science institute in Berlin, Germany. At first, Meitner was forced to work in a basement, away from the men! After a lot of effort and hard work, she became a respected scientist. Lise Meitner was the first person to realize that uranium atoms could be split to release radiation. She called this process **nuclear fission** (fission means splitting apart).

150 gallons (568 liters) of oil. The pellets are sealed inside metal fuel rods about 12 feet (3.66 meters) long, which fit into the center of the reactor core.

The chain reaction begins when neutrons are fired into the core from another radioactive source. They hit the uranium atoms in the fuel rods. The uranium atoms split, releasing heat energy and more neutrons. These neutrons fly out to hit and split more uranium nuclei. The heat produced by the chain reactions warms the liquid (usually water) surrounding the fuel rods. This liquid is called the **coolant.** Heat from the coolant is transferred to a set of pipes weaving through the core. The pipes contain water that changes to steam when it heats up. The steam spins the turbines that turn the generator to make electricity.

Controlling the chain reaction

How do engineers control the chain reaction in a nuclear reactor? They use long, thin cylinders called control rods. These rods catch extra neutrons zipping around, which prevents them from splitting more atoms. The reaction speeds up when the control rods are lifted out of the core. It slows down when the control rods are dropped into the core.

Keeping radiation in

We have seen how nuclear reactors release and control energy. They also have to

" . . . this new power, which has proved itself to be such a terrifying weapon of destruction, is harnessed for the first time for the common good of our community."

Queen Elizabeth II of Britain at the opening of the world's first commercial nuclear power plant, Calder Hall, Sellafield, England, 1956

contain that energy. Radiation from nuclear reactors must not escape. To prevent this, the reactor is surrounded by a thick steel or concrete structure called a containment vessel. During normal operation, this structure stops radiation from escaping. It also needs to be strong enough to stop radiation from escaping in case of an accident.

CHERNOBYL

In 1986, Unit 4 of the Chernobyl nuclear power plant in Ukraine exploded during a safety test. The nuclear fuel melted. The coolant water boiled and released steam. Steam pressure blew off the reactor roof and destroyed most of the reactor building. The nuclear core and fuel began burning. The fire burned itself out after two weeks. All the while, radiation escaped. Winds carried the radiation over Europe. Radiation even traveled to parts of the United States. Millions of people in Ukraine were exposed to high amounts of radiation. So far, about four thousand deaths have been linked to the accident.

Shortly after the accident, workers built a concrete container around the damaged reactor. That container is now crumbling. Workers are building a new covering for the reactor. It is only safe for them for minutes at a time.

The city of Pripyat, Ukraine, was created to house Chernobyl workers. Pripyat was abandoned completely after the accident. People left behind most possessions, including pets. No one can live there for hundreds of years.

Accidents

Nuclear reactors are built very carefully to prevent disasters. Still, accidents happen. In March 1979, a serious accident occurred at the Three Mile Island nuclear power plant near Harrisburg, Pennsylvania. A faulty pump and a stuck valve caused at least one-third of the coolant to drain from the reactor core. The core heated up and about half of the fuel rods melted. Engineers brought the reactor back under control. Later, some radioactive gases escaped into the air. No one was injured in the Three Mile Island accident.

The world's worst nuclear accident occurred at the Chernobyl nuclear power plant in Ukraine in Eastern Europe on April 26, 1986. The core melted. A cloud of radiation escaped. About fifty people died within days of the accident. Thousands more became sick or died from radiation exposure.

In 2005, the Sellafield nuclear fuel processing plant in England had an accident. Thousands of gallons (liters) of radioactive liquid drained from a broken pipe. The liquid did not escape from the plant, however. Nobody was injured. These kinds of accidents make people worry about using nuclear energy.

KEY WORDS

core: the part of a nuclear reactor that contains the fuel

generator: a machine that turns mechanical energy into electrical energy

nuclear reactor: a device in which controlled nuclear reactions take place

power plant: a factory that produces electricity

CHAPTER FOUR

USING NUCLEAR ENERGY

Nuclear power plants make clean energy. They can run all the time. These types of power plants produce huge amounts of electricity. They don't take up much space.

> "Without these nuclear plants, America would release nearly 700 million metric tons [or about 772 million tons] more carbon dioxide into the air each year. That's about the same amount of carbon dioxide that now comes from all our cars and trucks."
>
> President George W. Bush, speaking at Calvert Cliffs Nuclear Power Plant, Lusby, Maryland, June 22, 2005

Around the world

In 2006, thirty-one nations used nuclear power. There were more than four hundred nuclear reactors around the world. The United States has more nuclear reactors than any other nation. It produces about 20 percent of its electricity from nuclear energy — enough for California, Texas, and New York put together.

France gets more of its electricity from nuclear power than any other nation. It makes almost 80 percent of its electricity using nuclear energy.

Where nuclear power is used

The United States has 103 working nuclear power

plants at sixty-five locations around the country. Illinois, with six power plants, produces more nuclear energy than any other state. Pennsylvania and South Carolina are the other top producers. The energy produced in U.S. power plants supplies electricity to millions of homes and businesses.

We use nuclear reactors for other purposes, too. Nuclear reactors power many of the U.S. Navy's submarines and ships. Some spacecraft get electricity and heat from nuclear energy sources.

Dealing with waste

Power plants generate only a tiny amount of waste every year — about 1.3 cubic yards (1 cubic meter). **Radioactive** waste stays dangerous for thousands of years. Over time, it becomes weaker.

Region or country (Number of reactors in 2006)	
Western Europe	134
United States	103
Eastern Europe and Russia	70
Japan and Korea	75
India and Pakistan	18
Canada	18
China and Taiwan	16
Mexico, Argentina, and Brazil	6
South Africa	2

After ten years, **nuclear waste** has lost a little of its radioactivity — but it is still dangerous to handle. After five hundred years, the waste will be even less harmful.

Living things must be protected from nuclear waste. It must be tightly sealed and carefully stored. It must also be kept dry.

OUT IN SPACE

Spacecraft that must travel far from the Sun cannot rely on solar energy for power. They use **radioisotope thermoelectric generators** (RTGs) instead. An RTG makes electricity using the metal plutonium dioxide. Plutonium-238 (Pu-238) is radioactive. It produces heat inside the RTG, which makes electricity. *Cassini (left)* will need 600—700 watts of power at Saturn.

RTG

The *Cassini-Huygens* spacecraft carried three RTGs. The RTGs powered the spacecraft as it traveled to Saturn. It continues to explore the planet.

Scientists have researched ways to dispose of nuclear waste without harming living beings. Sending it into space was one idea. Scientists finally decided the safest place for radioactive material is deep underground.

YUCCA MOUNTAIN

Nuclear waste is currently stored at more than 120 different sites in the United States. Beginning in 2017, the Department of Energy is planning to bury all U.S. nuclear waste in one place — Yucca Mountain, Nevada. The nuclear waste will be sealed inside thick metal containers. The containers will be buried in dry rock about 1,000 feet (300 meters) below the surface.

Fear of nuclear power

Many Americans and people in other countries are afraid of nuclear power. It makes them think of nuclear bombs. They worry about being exposed to radiation. They are afraid of accidents and terrorist attacks at nuclear power plants. Some worry that nuclear waste cannot be stored safely.

For these reasons, few nuclear power plants have been built in the United States in recent years. In the next decade or so, that is going to change.

KEY WORDS

nuclear waste: the radioactive by-product, or waste, of nuclear energy production

radioactive: able to produce radiation

radioisotope thermo-electric generator (RTG): a device that makes electricity from the heat produced by the radioactive material plutonium–238

CHAPTER FIVE

THE FUTURE OF NUCLEAR ENERGY

Many people are worried about global warming. Nuclear energy can reduce greenhouse gases and produce electricity cleanly. Countries around the world are building new nuclear power plants. Scientists are working to make the production of nuclear energy safer.

New reactors

After about thirty years, most nuclear reactors themselves have become radioactive. The building and its materials are considered nuclear waste.

New types of reactors may replace some of the older designs. A **breeder reactor** is a nuclear power plant that makes more fuel than it uses. A breeder reactor reprocesses (reuses) its spent fuel. Older breeder reactors are less safe than regular reactors. Improved designs for breeder reactors will make them safer. They should reduce waste, too.

New types of power plants, including nuclear reactors, should be able to run on the same amounts of fuel as today's power plants. But they will produce more electricity. They may also produce hydrogen gas as a by-product. Like electricity, hydrogen can be used for power. In the future, it may become common to use hydrogen instead of gasoline to fuel cars and to heat homes and office buildings.

PORTABLE POWER

Navies around the world use portable nuclear reactors to provide fuel to power their ships. U.S. engineers are developing SSTAR, a compact breeder reactor small enough to use almost anywhere. SSTAR measures about 15 feet (5 meters) and 9 feet (3 meters) high. Instead of water, SSTAR will use liquid metal as a coolant. Each unit will generate electricity for thirty years and can be recycled.

Nuclear fusion

Future power plants may use a type of nuclear reaction called **nuclear fusion**. Fusion means joining together. In nuclear fusion, the nuclei of atoms join together to form new atoms with larger nuclei.

Nuclear fusion powers our Sun. It uses hydrogen as its fuel. Heat and pressure inside the Sun squeeze hydrogen nuclei together to make helium nuclei. Huge amounts of radiation are released in this reaction. This radiation includes heat and light. Fusion reactors would use hydrogen to create nuclear energy.

Fusion dangers

A hydrogen bomb is a fusion reaction. These bombs are even more powerful than the atomic bombs used to end World War II. In 1952, the U.S. tested its first hydrogen bomb. The huge explosion destroyed Enewetak Atoll in the Pacific Ocean. It left a crater 164 feet (50 meters) deep.

THE FIRST FUSION REACTOR

The International Thermonuclear Experimental Reactor (ITER) is a project involving many nations. The United States, China, India, Japan, South Korea, and the countries of the European Union and the Russian Federation are supporting the $13 billion project. In 2006, the nations agreed on a site — Cadarache, France. Construction on the ITER fusion reactor will take many years. Scientists hope to have it working by 2016.

ITER fusion reactor (cutaway view)

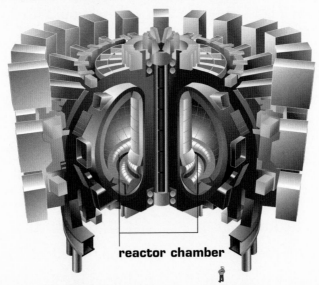

reactor chamber

human figure to show size

The central chamber of a fusion reactor is shaped like a doughnut. This shape — called a tokamak — allows extremely hot gases (plasma) to spin around at high rates of speed without touching the chamber's sides.

While hydrogen bombs are meant to explode, nuclear power plants must not. A nuclear fusion power plant would use extremely high temperatures. Such heat turns the fuel into a gas-like state of matter called **plasma**. Plasma consists of high-energy, electrically charged particles. It is kept under high pressure in a doughnut-shaped reactor. The plasma is kept spinning so fast that it does not touch the sides of the reactor. If it did, the sides would melt. Heat from the plasma is transferred to a set of pipes. Water in the pipes is turned to steam, which turns the turbines of the power plant.

Scientists do not expect to make fusion a common source of energy until about the middle of this century. When they do, we may have an endless supply of electricity.

Part of the picture

Fears about nuclear energy remain, but our energy needs continue to grow. We must find new ways to meet those increasing needs. Oil, gas, and coal will someday run out. It will be a long time before people can depend on renewable sources such as water, wind, and solar energy for all their power. We may find that nuclear energy is also an important fuel for the future.

KEY WORDS

breeder reactor: a nuclear reactor that reprocesses its fuel to make new fuel

nuclear fusion: a nuclear reaction in which atomic nuclei fuse, or join together

plasma: a very hot mixture of gases that can conduct electricity

GLOSSARY

atoms: tiny particles that make up all matter

chain reaction: a reaction that sets off other reactions

coolant: a substance that cools another nearby substance without mixing

element: a pure substance that cannot be separated and contains atoms of only one type

generator: a machine that turns mechanical energy into electrical energy

global warming: the gradual warming of Earth's climate

nuclear fission: a nuclear reaction in which atomic nuclei break apart

nuclear fusion: a nuclear reaction in which atomic nuclei fuse, or join together

nuclear reaction: a change to an atom's nucleus that creates energy

nuclear waste: a radioactive by-product (leftover) from a nuclear reaction

nucleus: a cluster of neutrons and protons at the center of an atom. Nuclei is the plural form.

plasma: a very hot mixture of liquified gases that can conduct electricity

power plant: a factory that produces electricity

radiation: the energy given off by atoms in the form of invisible waves and particles

radioactive: able to produce radiation

radioisotope thermo-electric generator (RTG): a device that makes electricity from the heat produced by the radioactive material plutonium-238

TOP EIGHT ENERGY SOURCES

The following list highlights the major fuel sources of the twenty-first century.
It also lists some advantages and disadvantages of each:

	Advantages	Disadvantages
Biofuels	renewable energy source; widely available from a number of sources, including farms, restaurants, and everday garbage	fossil fuels often used to grow farm crops; requires special processing facilities that run on fossil fuels in order to produce usable biofuel
Fossil fuels: coal, oil, petroleum	used by functioning power plants worldwide; supports economies	limited supplies; emit greenhouse gases; produce toxic wastes; must often be transported long distances
Geothermal energy	nonpolluting; renewable; free source	only available in localized areas; would require redesign of heating systems
Hydrogen (fuel cells)	most abundant element in the universe; nonpolluting	production of fuel cells uses up fossil fuels; hydrogen gas storage presents safety issues
Nuclear energy	produces no greenhouse gases; produces a lot of energy from small amounts of fuel	solid wastes remain dangerous for centuries; limited life span of power plants
Solar power	renewable; produces no pollutants; free source	weather and climate dependent; solar cells expensive to manufacture
Water power	renewable resource; generally requires no additional fuel	requires flowing water, waves, or tides; can interfere with view; dams may destroy large natural areas and disrupt human settlements
Wind power	renewable; nonpolluting; free source	depends on weather patterns; depends on location; endangers bird populations

RESOURCES

Books

Crewe, Sabrina and Dale Anderson.
The Atom Bomb Project.
Events That Shaped America (series).
Gareth Stevens Publishing (2005)

Walker, Linda.
Living After Chernobyl.
Children in Crisis (series).
World Almanac Library (2006)

Web Sites

www.eia.doe.gov/kids/energyfacts/ sources/non-renewable/nuclear.html
Find out more about nuclear energy at the U.S. Department of Energy's nuclear power Web site.

www.nrc.gov/reading-rm/basic-ref/students.html
Explore the Students' Corner of the U.S. Nuclear Regulatory Commission's Web site.

Publisher's note to educators and parents: Our editors have carefully reviewed these Web sites to ensure that they are suitable for children. Many Web sites change frequently, however, and we cannot guarantee that a site's future contents will continue to meet our high standards of quality and educational value. Be advised that children should be closely supervised whenever they access the Internet.

INDEX